The Anointing: The Glory of God

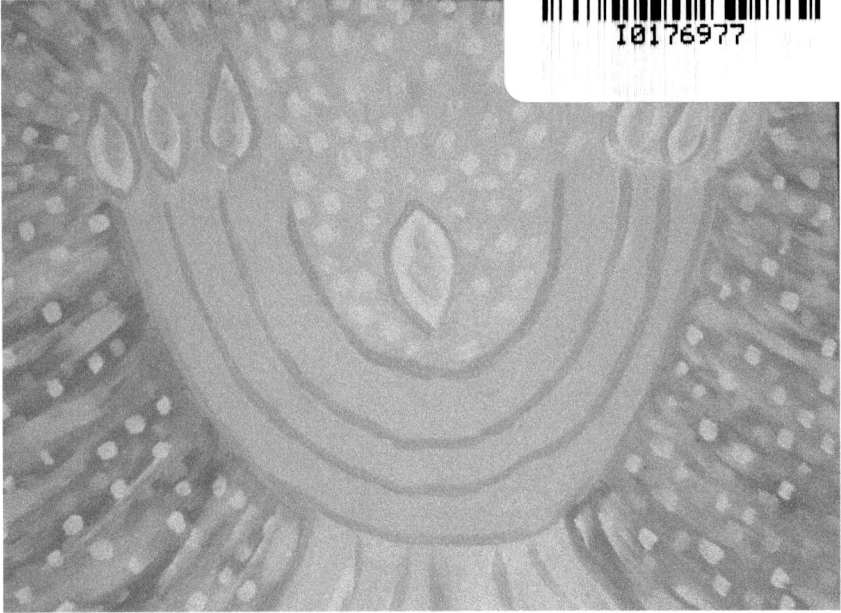

CHRIS A. LEGEBOW

CHRIS A. LEGEBOW

ISBN - 978-0-9952715-4-8

DEDICATION

I thank God for the churches I have been privileged to be a part of. I thank God for the Macchiavello family for adopting me. I thank God for those who have shared their testimonies of God's miraculous dealings in their lives. I thank God for the Christian media broadcasting Apostles, Prophets, Pastors, Teachers, and Evangelists. I especially thank God for His Holy Spirit. I have known the presence of the most high God and soaked in the beauty of His Spirit and known the ecstasy of His presence. I am more passionate about God today than ever because of His continual drawing of me closer to Him. I pray that God may give you, reader, a desire for more of Him, that you may know the glory of God in your life – the anointing to serve the LORD Jesus Christ.

CONTENTS

ACKNOWLEDGMENTS

All Scripture taken from Biblegateway.com
Modern English Version (MEV) 2017.

1 INTRODUCTION

The Anointing

Even if you have recently become a born again Christian, you will know the term "The Anointing". This teaching is going to explain what it is and what it isn't and what it is for and why it is important. Examples from the Old Testament and New Testament are given. It is my hope that you will want more of God that you may be transformed into His image and likeness. It is my desire that you will treasure God's presence and thank Him for His presence – the glory of God living on the inside of you Christian.

God's Presence

The anointing in the Old Testament is very different from the anointing in the new testament. The anointing is the presence of God upon a person to quicken that person in the gifts of the Holy Spirit or for Divine service. In the Old Testament, people who worshipped God only knew Him from a distance. Because of the sin of Adam and Eve, people were born in sin. The only way to approach God was with worship and the slaying of an animal (sheep) to cover our sins to make it possible for God to have any type of relationship with us. Sin separates you from God. The animal's blood did not forgive sin; it only covered the sin. It was not possible for any person to approach God without a sacrifice of blood.

Moses and the Ark of the Covenant

Moses knew the presence of God more than any other person. He was instructed by God to build the ark of the covenant for the commandments and to be a dwelling place for the presence of God. God's presence was in that ark. Touching the ark could mean immanent death. As Moses or Aaron, the high priest would approach the ark worshipping God, the glory of God would fill the tabernacle. The glory of God was so bright that it is visible as a glory light on the tabernacle. Most people feared the presence of God because God hates sin, and if there was sin, the person would die.

Hebrews 12: 22 But you have come to Mount Zion and to the city of the living God, the heavenly Jerusalem, and to an innumerable company of angels; 23 to the general assembly and church of the firstborn, who are enrolled in heaven; to God, the Judge of all; and to the spirits of the righteous ones made perfect.

The High Priest

The high priest would make sacrifice for his own sin before interceding or praying for God to forgive others. All people revered and feared the presence of God. Only certain people heard God speak to them. Only certain people had the anointing of the Holy Spirit upon them. God would rest His presence on a person, usually a prophet of God and there would be a manifestation of the glory of God. God would speak with the prophets or show them visions or instruct them concerning Israel. Often miracles occurred in the earth because of these faithful people who served and worshipped the one true God. They would speak to the people and give God's instructions and God's answers concerning major events or things important to the people. This could be compared to pouring oil over a person and totally covering the person. Aaron the high priest had to be sprinkled with both oil and blood. The way oil clings to a person's body is the way the Holy Spirit would rest upon a person. It could be compared to a trained white dove – I choose white for holiness. The dove would sit upon a person and go away and return and sit upon a person. So was the presence of God upon those who served and honoured Jehovah.

Once the Temple was built in Jerusalem, there was an outer court, a Holy place and the inner most region called the Holy of Holies; the ark of the covenant was there in the Holy of Holies. A thick curtain separated the Holy place or place of offering praise from the most Holy place. Only the high priest could enter the Holy of Holies once a year to offer sacrifice for the sins of the people. It was such a Holy place that the high priest would have a rope with bells tied to his ankle so that as long as people in the Holy place could hear the tinkling of the bells, they knew the high priest was received and well. If the bells stopped, it would mean the priest had sin and died there; the people could pull him out by the rope.

The ark of the Covenant was a constant reminder to the people of Israel of God's Holiness and their need for a Saviour. They expected the Messiah but when Jesus came, they did not know him or accept him. When Jesus died on the cross the thick curtain or veil that separated the Holy of Holies from the Holy place (in the Temple) was torn from the top to the bottom. This was to show the people that Messiah had come and no longer would they have to be separate or distant from God.

Matthew 27: 51 At that moment the curtain of the temple was torn in two, from the top to the bottom. And the ground shook, and the rocks split apart. 52 The graves also were opened, and many bodies of the saints who had died were raised, 53 and coming out of the graves after His resurrection, they went into the Holy City and appeared to many.

The people did not understand what had happened until God revealed it to them afterwards. No longer was an animal sacrifice needed to approach God. Faith in the blood of Jesus washes and cleanses a person from sin. I mean it is just as if the person never sinned. This truth is taught with the title of Justification in the Christian Church. It is essential the person approach God thanking Him for the blood of Jesus and expressing faith in God's sacrifice Jesus Christ, the lamb of God that takes away the sin of the world (John 1: 29). No longer is there a distance between the dwelling place of God and the people who worship God.

Jesus promised this present Spirit of God with us as He spoke to his disciples. He promised something that had never been given before. He promised the Holy Spirit would come and teach us, guide us, and live with us.

John 14: 15 "If you love Me, keep My commandments. 16 I will pray the Father, and He will give you another Counselor, that He may be with you forever: 17 the Spirit of truth, whom the world cannot receive, for it does not see Him, neither does it know Him. But you know Him, for He lives with you, and will be in you.

John 16: 7 Nevertheless I tell you the truth: It is expedient for you that I go away. For if I do not go away, the Counselor will not come to you. But if I go, I will send Him to you. 8 When He comes, He will convict the world of sin and of righteousness and of judgment: 9 of sin, because they do not believe in Me; 10 of righteousness, because I am going to My Father, and you will see Me no more; 11 and of judgment, because the ruler of this world stands condemned.

Luke 24: 48 You are witnesses of these things. 49 And look, I am sending the promise of My Father upon you. But wait in the city of Jerusalem until you are clothed with power from on high."

3

Acts 1: 8 But you shall receive power when the Holy Spirit comes upon you. And you shall be My witnesses in Jerusalem, and in all Judea and Samaria, and to the ends of the earth."

The Presence of God in the New Testament

In the New Testament, God's presence is revealed in a different way because of Jesus. God the Holy Spirit comes to reside inside of a person who believes in the LORD Jesus Christ. God lives on the inside of us. His Spirit is a permanent companion. Every place that I go, I bring the Holy Spirit with me. God living in us was only made possible because of Jesus Christ who lived a holy life, died on a cross for our sins, rose from the dead and ascended into heaven. Faith in Jesus Christ's blood shed for our sins, is the essential belief of the Christian faith. He died for us so that we might live eternally and have communion with God.

Jesus blood cleanses us from all sin and unrighteousness so we can directly speak with God.

1 John 1: 9 If we confess our sins, He is faithful and just to forgive us our sins and cleanse us from all unrighteousness.

After Jesus ascended into heaven, the disciples gathered in the upper room in Jerusalem as Jesus had instructed them. They waited and prayed not exactly knowing what it was but that Jesus promised to send His Holy Spirit. After a period of praying and waiting for what God promised suddenly their lives were changed completely.

Acts 2: 2 When the day of Pentecost had come, they were all together in one place. 2 Suddenly a sound like a mighty rushing wind came from heaven, and it filled the whole house where they were sitting. 3 There appeared to them tongues as of fire, being distributed and resting on each of them, 4 and they were all filled with the Holy Spirit and began to speak in other tongues, as the Spirit enabled them to speak.

Never has it been recorded that this occurred again the exact same way. There was, in a closed room, a mighty rushing wind. There was a physical manifestation of God's presence that appeared as flames above the heads of the disciples. They began speaking in other languages they had never studied. The presence of God was so strong on them that it compelled them to go into the street below. They continued worshipping and speaking in these tongues of the Holy Spirit in the streets of Jerusalem.

There were pilgrims gathered to worship God on the day of Pentecost. They came from other nations to Israel. The disciples loudly praising God and worshipping God in tongues gathered a crowd. People from different nations proclaimed that they were speaking in the language of their countries.

Acts 2: 7 They were all amazed and marveled, saying to each other, "Are not all these who are speaking Galileans? 8 How is it that we hear, each in our own native language? 9 Parthians, Medes and Elamites, residents of Mesopotamia, Judea and Cappadocia, Pontus and Asia, 10 Phrygia and Pamphylia, Egypt and the regions of Libya near Cyrene, and visitors from Rome, both Jews and proselytes, 11 Cretans and Arabs—we hear them speaking in our own languages the mighty works of God." 12 They were all amazed and perplexed, saying to each other, "What does this mean?"

Some mocked it and accused the disciples as being drunk. But others testified it was their language being spoken and God was being worshipped. The Apostle Peter could not hold back. He began to preach what this evidence of speaking in other tongues meant. He by the Spirit of God prophesied speaking with wisdom beyond all natural wisdom. He recognized the presence of God that day fulfilling a prophecy of Joel from the Old Testament.

Acts 2: 16 But this is what was spoken by the prophet Joel:

17 'In the last days it shall be,' says God,
    'that I will pour out My Spirit on all flesh;
your sons and your daughters shall prophesy,
    your young men shall see visions,
    and your old men shall dream dreams.
18 Even on My menservants and maidservants
    I will pour out My Spirit in those days;
    and they shall prophesy.

God's Spirit was poured out upon the people. Peter preached the truth of Jesus as Messiah his death, burial, resurrection and ascension according to the Scriptures. He quoted how Jesus had fulfilled these prophecies. It so moved the crowd that was gathered that they believed that Jesus was Messiah and they wanted to know what they should do.

Peter answered them with words not only for them but for all the ages to come.

Acts 2: 38 Peter said to them, "Repent and be baptized, every one of you, in the name of Jesus Christ for the forgiveness of sins, and you shall receive the gift of the Holy Spirit. 39 For the promise is to you, and to your children, and to all who are far away, as many as the Lord our God will call."

The Baptism of the Holy Spirit is for all Believers

Clearly, Peter had been enlightened by God to realize that the Baptism of the Holy Spirit was for all people who believed on Jesus as Messiah. This day marked the beginning of the Pentecostal movement on the earth. It was taught to all the generations to follow. That day over 3, 000 people accepted Jesus as Messiah and were baptized in the Holy Spirit. Please note, the special description of physical flames upon a person appearing was never repeated, but the same Holy Spirit that filled them and compelled them to preach Christ is the same Holy Spirit that comes to dwell in us. Jesus Christ baptizes you in the Holy Spirit and there is evidence of speaking with other tongues.

How to Receive the Baptism of the Holy Spirit

The same is true today. To be saved and baptized in the Holy Spirit, a person must repent or turn away from sins towards God; believe that Jesus died for all sins and receive forgiveness of sins and the Baptism of the Holy Spirit with the evidence of speaking in new tongues. There are different manifestations of tongues. The gift of tongues means the person can pray in an unknown language or a language only known to God. Interpretation of tongues the gift is given to proclaim the meaning of the tongues. Sometimes there is a special gifting of the Holy Spirit to speak prophetically in languages of the earth the person has not studied. This same gift is present in the church today and has been documented.

One of my former pastors, who is a mighty prophet of God, would sometimes be praying for people or prophesying and suddenly start speaking Spanish. He had not studied Spanish at that time but people in the congregation came and spoke to him what he had said. Often it was encouragement and the speaking of scriptures from the Bible. The same Holy Spirit empowers believers for service to preach Christ by other spiritual gifts. They are mentioned here. There are three types of gifts of the Spirit: motivational, manifestational and Ministry. This is a topic of a different study.

1 Corinthians 12: 7 But the manifestation of the Spirit is given to everyone for the common good. 8 To one is given by the Spirit the word of wisdom, to another the word of knowledge by the same Spirit, 9 to another faith by the same Spirit, to another gifts of healings by the same Spirit, 10 to another the working of miracles, to another prophecy, to another discerning of spirits, to another various kinds of tongues, and to another the interpretation of tongues. 11 But that one and very same Spirit works all these, dividing to each one individually as He will.

The Evidence of Speaking in Tongues

The evidence of speaking in tongues is only one evidence. There are other gifts of the Spirit and other manifestations such as trembling or physical shaking of the body, crying or weeping with thanksgiving, being slain in the Spirit – being overwhelmed by God's presence in such a way that the person falls to the ground with the presence of God very strong on the person. The person does not even feel himself or herself falling and there is never any injury. To explain it would be to say that the strength of the Holy Spirit is too overwhelming for a human being to stand in.

The evidences of the Holy Spirit is not the whole of His indwelling presence only a manifestation or outward sign of it. The Holy Spirit comes to live in us not only for manifestations (that lead us to witness for Jesus), but also to transform us from glory to glory.

2 Corinthians 3: 18 But we all, seeing the glory of the Lord with unveiled faces, as in a mirror, are being transformed into the same image from glory to glory by the Spirit of the Lord.

I literally mean that as clay is softened and changed by adding water or adding more clay, the substance itself changes. The person is changed to be more like Christ. The more a person pursues God, the more God manifests His glory towards the person. God does not make you seek Him. Each person may choose to pursue God. The anointing is not all of the Holy Spirit. The Holy Spirit is a person – a part of the Triune God - who lives in believers and does many different things such as teach us, lead us, guide us, correct us, etc. The Holy Spirit could be the topic of a different study.

This book will cover some of the manifestations of the Holy Spirit's anointing in the Old Testament, and in the New Testament. I believe there is nothing insignificant in the Old Testament. It is God's word for us as much as the New Testament is. It is either there to show us something in the New Testament or a pattern that is repeated etc. May God quicken the words to you so that you might treasure the Holy Spirit's presence in your life more than ever.

2 THE ANOINTING OF DAVID

David was the last in a line of brothers to Jesse. He was a shepherd and just a young boy in this passage. The prophet Samuel goes there at God's command. God told Samuel he was displeased with Saul and wanted to anoint a new king (this is while Saul is still king). Jesse lines up his sons for the prophet to choose and as Samuel approaches each one, he notices things such as strength, height, rugged, handsome appearance etc.

1 Samuel 16: 7 But the Lord said to Samuel, "Do not look on his appearance or on the height of his stature, because I have rejected him. For the Lord sees not as man sees. For man looks on the outward appearance, but the Lord looks on the heart."

God speaks to him during his examination of each son and says not this one. Samuel has examined each one but none of them is God's choice. As Samuel is praying discerning the LORD, he enquires if all sons are there.

1 Samuel 16: Samuel said to Jesse, "The Lord has not chosen these." 11 Samuel said to Jesse, "Are these all your young men?"

Jesse says there is one more but he is a boy. He is a shepherd. In other words, he wasn't even considered worthy to count in the line up. Samuel commands that he be brought to him. David is handsome with reddish hair but a youth. As soon as Samuel sees him, the Holy Spirit reveals to him that he is the chosen one.

1 Samuel 16: 12 So he sent and brought him [David] in. Now he was ruddy with beautiful eyes and a good appearance. And the Lord said, "Arise, anoint him, for this is he."

The LORD spoke to Samuel. He was the only one hearing from God in that room. The instruction was directly from the LORD. At the command of the LORD, Samuel took a horn of oil and poured it over David anointing him to be the next king of Israel.

1 Samuel 16: 13 Then Samuel took the horn of oil, and anointed him in the midst of his brothers. And the Spirit of the Lord came on David from that day forward. So Samuel arose and went to Ramah.

The Anointing Oil

The oil of anointing was a symbolic representation as to what was going on spiritually. The anointing to be king was upon David. It was a way of God showing favour. It was a day that no one who witnessed it could deny. Something special had happened that day. Samuel departed. Life seemed to go on as normal for David and his family. Saul was still the king. God was anointing him to prepare him for leadership. God was setting him apart from his family and consecrating him unto Himself. God's Spirit came on David in a special way from that day; he was told he was to be the king of Israel. All of life seemed normal afterwards but it wasn't the same. God had placed His Spirit upon David. Samuel had specific direct instruction from God.

Although Saul is still the king, he is in disobedient to the LORD so the LORD removed His presence from Saul. Because of Saul's disobedience, God places the anointing to be king on someone else – David. It is not that the oil itself is Holy or magical. The oil is a representation of what was occurring in the spiritual realm – a transferring of the anointing for leadership upon David. The oil was used for a Holy purpose. Faith in the action of the Prophet pouring the oil over him and prophesying he would be king is what is especially sacred. It was not done lightly. God Himself directed the anointing.

The Anointing Brings new Opportunities.

The anointing of God came on David that day in a new way. He knew a new level of blessing upon his life. He was not immediately king. It was not to occur for at least 17 more years or longer. David began to get favour with people. He began to become popular and to stand out. Remember he wasn't even asked to stand with his brothers in the line up because none of them considered him to be a choice. Soon afterwards, he is selected to play the harp and sing for King Saul.

What had happened was that an evil spirit had come upon Saul. As David would sing and play the harp, the evil spirit would depart. The anointing on David brought peace to Saul. What happened to Saul was terrible. His willful disobedience to God caused God to remove His blessing, His anointing from Saul; this made a kind of spiritual void that caused an evil spirit to possess him. The same thing could happen to someone today. Willful sin, and refusal to repent can invite demons to possess a person. I do believe that had Saul repented with all his heart, God would have shown mercy to him. Saul did not repent of his sin. He acknowledged it but did not repent of it. Saul cares about what people think about him and outward appearances, but he does not care about what God thinks.

If we fail to honour or revere the LORD as God and try to go our own sinful way without repenting, God will remove His blessing from our lives. God had instructed Saul through Samuel to completely kill all the Amalekites including all the animals. God gave specific instruction. Saul mostly obeyed but decided to keep some sheep and cattle because they looked good. He did not kill Agag the king. God's instructions were clear and Saul did not fully obey. Samuel had instructed Saul to wait for him to come and place a blessing on a sacrifice to thank God for the victory. Saul did not obey. When Samnuel comes to him, Saul believes he is innocent and that he had fully obeyed the LORD. He welcomes Samuel saying he has kept the word of God.

Samuel's famous words 1 Samuel 15: 4 Samuel said, "Then what is the sound of this flock of sheep in my ears? And the sound of the cattle which I am hearing?"

Saul admits he kept some of the herds of animals for sacrifices. He admits he did not kill Agag. He confesses his sin. 24 Saul said to Samuel, "I have sinned. For I have transgressed the commandment of the Lord, and your words, because I feared the people, and obeyed their voice. 25 Now therefore, please pardon my sin and return with me, that I may worship the Lord."

Samuel's words are God's condemnation of him. 26 Samuel said to Saul, "I will not return with you. For you have rejected the word of the Lord, and the Lord has rejected you from being king over Israel."

Please notice. Saul does not repent. He does not humble himself before God even though he admits he has sinned. Because he fears what the people think he begs Samuel to do a sacrifice with him.

1 Samuel 15: 30 Then he said, "I have sinned, yet please honor me before the elders of my people, and before Israel, and turn back with me, that I may worship the Lord your God." 31 So Samuel turned back after Saul, and Saul worshipped the Lord.

He cared about the outward appearance of the day – not about his sin towards God. God is so merciful, I believe if Saul would have truly realized his sin and repented and asked God to forgive him, God would have done it. I want to explain to you why I believe this. The most wicked king mentioned in the Old Testament is King Ahab. He murdered, plundered, served false gods etc. He most certainly did not follow God for almost all of his life.

The Prophet Elijah Pronounces Horrible Judgement on Ahab.

1 Kings 21: And he answered, "I have found you, because you have sold yourself to work evil in the sight of the Lord. 21 'See, I will bring disaster upon you and will take away your posterity and will cut off all your males, both free and slave, who are left in Israel, 22 and will make your house like the house of Jeroboam the son of Nebat and like the house of Baasha the son of Ahijah, for the provocation with which you have provoked Me to anger and made Israel to sin.'

23 "The Lord also spoke of Jezebel, saying, 'The dogs will eat Jezebel by the wall of Jezreel.'

24 "Those from Ahab's family who die in the city will be eaten by dogs, and those who die in the field will be eaten by birds of the air."

A prophet pronouncing such a severe judgement means most certainly there was to be consequence for all his years of sinning.

1 Kings 21: 27 When Ahab heard those words, he tore his clothes and put on sackcloth on his flesh and fasted and lay in sackcloth and walked meekly.

28 The word of the Lord came to Elijah the Tishbite, saying, 29 "See how Ahab humbles himself before Me? Because he humbles himself before Me, I will not bring the disaster during his lifetime, but during his son's lifetime I will bring the disaster on his household."

If God can show such mercy over the most wicked sinful king, I believe he would have showed mercy on Saul had he repented.

3 THE ANOINTING MANIFESTS GLORY

Spirit of Prophecy

A different example of the anointing is Saul. It is a peculiar aspect of the anointing. It is connected to the spirit of prophecy. Many people will not understand this because they will not have experienced it, but a strong spiritual moving of the LORD can come on a group of prophets as they gather. As a company of prophets gather, expectation for hearing from God and faith to prophesy fills the atmosphere. The glory of God can be so strong in such a meeting that people tremble or fall to the ground with the glory of God overflowing in them.

That would be peculiar in itself, but in this instance Saul, who has an evil spirit upon him who is filled with jealousy and hatred for David wants to kill David. Saul realizes that he has lost the anointing of the LORD and that David has it [but he does not repent] hates David because of it. Saul orders some of his servants to go kill David. Jonathon, his son (David's friend) reasons with Saul that it David, the captain of Saul's army, (promoted by Saul) has only been a faithful, servant to Saul. Saul is calmed by Jonathon but only briefly. David slew Goliath' David was the captain of the army because God's favour was on him to win battles for Israel. As usual, one day Saul is dining with David, who was a loyal, trustworthy servant but that one day changed David's life forever.

1 Samuel 19: 9 Now an evil spirit from the Lord was upon Saul as he was sitting in his house with his spear in his hand. And David was playing the lyre. 10 Then Saul sought to pin David to the wall with the spear, but he escaped from Saul's presence. He struck the spear into the wall. But David fled and escaped that night.

David understood that Saul wanted to kill him. I don't believe he understood fully why but he certainly wasn't going to stay there knowing his life was threatened. Saul had given David one of his daughters Michael to be his wife. Saul sent servants there to kill David. Saul's own family were defending David and helping him escape. David escaped to Ramah one of the cities of refuge. This was a place that if anyone had committed a crime but not on purpose, he or she could go there and live until the high priest died. It was a place of protection of amnesty. God had appointed several such cities to be built in Israel. Although it seems like a good solution,

David was on the run, without his family and friends, fearing for his life, not knowing why, innocent of any crime. He meets with Samuel and Samuel brings him to Naoith (in Ramah) where there was a company of prophets.

The atmosphere would have been encouraging, faith building and strengthening. David knew Samuel had anointed him to be king. Samuel knew David was innocent of any crimes against Saul. Samuel knew the Spirit of God had left Saul and been placed on David. David was there in a spiritual atmosphere when guards from Saul came to kill him. What happened was the anointing to prophesy was so strong there, the presence of God was so strong there, that it affected the guards. This happened on three occasions.

In 1 Samuel 19: 20 Then Saul sent messengers to take David, but when they saw the company of the prophets prophesying and Samuel taking his stand over them, the Spirit of God came upon the messengers of Saul and they also prophesied.

The anointing or presence of God was so strong, it came on those who came in. The guards started prophesying and worshipping God. This angered Saul so much he decided to go on his own to kill David. He had an evil spirit that wanted to kill David. You can reason with a person but you cannot reason with someone possessed by an evil spirit. [You command it to leave in the name of Jesus.] an evil spirit cannot just possess a person. The person has to have an entrance point. Unconfessed sin, evil doings, pagan worship – any of these things could be an entrance for an evil spirit to possess a person.

1 Samuel 19: 23 He went there to Naioth in Ramah, and the Spirit of God came upon him also. And he went on and he prophesied until he came to Naioth in Ramah. 24 He stripped off his clothes and he also prophesied before Samuel. And he lay down naked all that day and all that night. Therefore, they say, "Is Saul also among the prophets?"

The Spirit of Prophesy came on Saul

The Spirit of God was so strong there that Saul began to prophesy. The spirit of God is so strong that no evil spirit can come against it. I don't believe that God caused Saul to take off all his clothes but I do believe it has strong symbolic meaning. I believe the evil spirit in Saul would have tried to resist God's Spirit. It caused him to take off all his clothes, all his royal robes, symbolic of his authority. It is as though all his authority as a king was stripped away from him. What is somewhat fascinating here is that the Spirit of prophesy came upon Saul and caused him to prophesy also. All of this occurs, Saul does not repent.

4 THE PRESENCE OF GOD

The Tangible Presence of God

Moses God's servant who spoke with God as a man would speak with a friend had a special relationship with God and knew the Holy presence of God like no other person. He received commandments from God after delivering Israel out of Egypt after 400 years of slavery. All of Moses' relationship with God has some tangible presence. God appears to Moses first in a burning bush (Exodus 3). God causes signs and wonders to follow Moses ministry as he speaks to Pharaoh to let the slaves go free by command of the God I AM THAT I AM. We use the word Jehovah to explain that aspect of God as eternal. God delivers Israel out of Egypt, parts the Red Sea (Exodus 14) and saves Israel while drowning the Egyptians who chased them. Moses through all of Israel over 2 million people to Mt Sinai as commanded by God. This should have been a huge worship party by everyone there thanking God for all the miracles and freedom. Moses goes to speak with God by climbing the mountain. God gives Moses the commandments with tables of stone God Himself carved out of the rock and inscribed. This encounter with God was so extreme that it had tangible results on Moses' appearance.

Exodus 34: 29 When Moses came down from Mount Sinai with the two tablets of testimony in the hands of Moses, when he came down from the mountain, Moses did not know that the skin of his face shone while he talked with Him. 30 So when Aaron and all the children of Israel saw Moses, amazingly, the skin of his face shone, and they were afraid to come near him.

The people feared Moses because of the glory of God shining on Moses. Because of this, Moses wore a veil over his face when talking to people. The glory that came upon him was the same glory that was on the ark of the covenant that Moses had built according to God's command. God's Holy Spirit radiates light, glory.

I have been in services where the anointing of God is so strong on a preacher, an apostle or a prophet that there is a glory around the person. I didn't see with my natural eyes but with my spirit. There have been instances though in the New Covenant where places appeared as glowing or as lit up such as Azusa Street in 1906 or on Brother Branham who was a prophet of God (1950's). There are photos of him with a glowing light over him. Preachers or teachers with the anointing of God will appear larger than life. That is their words will directly impact your inner most being. Their faces may appear beautiful.

It is because God is filling that person from the inside. The person who lead me to the LORD was prophesying over me (I didn't know what that was) and he appeared almost as an angel to me. It was hard for me to believe he was human. He was saying things only I knew and that God knew. I knew that I knew his words were from God. I was unsaved but at the point where God could reach me. He used that man to speak the things of my heart so I would repent and receive Jesus. I did.

David

David knew the glory of God through his worship songs and his encounters with the prophets. God's spirit was upon him for worship and praise. David respected the ark of God and danced upon bringing it home after it had been captured. David celebrated the return of the ark of God knowing it was God's presence and blessing upon Israel.

1 Chronicles 16: 16 So they brought in the ark of God, placed it in the midst of the tent that David had erected for it, and drew near to God with burnt offerings and peace offerings. 2 When David had finished offering the burnt offerings and the peace offerings, he blessed the people in the name of the Lord. 3

He had a place built a place for the ark known as the Tabernacle of David and appointed many Levites to offer worship and praise and sacrifice before the ark day and night (I Chronicles 16: 39-42). The ark of the covenant held the commandments. It was an expression of God's love and commitment towards Israel. It gave them a place to worship and praise and offer sacrifices to God. It was as close as they could get to God. God was not in them but His Spirited rested on the ark.

Solomon

David had wanted to build a temple for God but God instructed him through the prophet Nathan that he should not but that his son Solomon should. God gave David all of the plans for the Temple that God had given to him. God gave David instructions about the temple so that for the rest of his life he gathered materials including gold and silver and precious jewels that would go towards the building of the Temple. David instructed

Solomon that his task was to build the Temple of God as God had commanded.

Upon the Building of the Temple, Solomon Offers up Prayer of Dedication to God.

1 Kings 8: 29 that Your eyes may be upon this house night and day, even toward the place of which You have said, 'My name shall be there,' that You may listen to the prayer which Your servant shall make toward this place. 30 Please listen to the supplication of Your servant and of Your people Israel when they pray toward this place. May You hear in heaven, Your dwelling place, and when You hear, forgive.

God places a Special Anointing on the Temple as Described in this Passage:

2 Chronicles 5: 11 When the priests came out from the Most Holy Place— for all the priests who were present had consecrated themselves, without keeping separate divisions— 12 and all the Levitical singers, Asaph, Heman, and Jeduthun, with their sons and relatives, all clothed in fine linen, with cymbals, harps, and lyres, stood to the east of the altar, and with them one hundred and twenty priests who were sounding with trumpets, 13 it happened, when the trumpet players and singers made one sound to praise and give thanks to the Lord, and when they lifted up their voice with the trumpets and cymbals and all the instruments of music and praised the Lord saying,

"For He is good
and His mercy endures forever,"

that the house, the house of the Lord, was filled with a cloud. 14 And the priests were not able to stand in order to serve because of the cloud, for the glory of the Lord had filled the house of God.

Literally, the glory of God was so strong on the ark of the covenant and in Israel's obedience to worship and offer sacrifices of animals of praise and worship that no one could stand in the Temple. They were overwhelmed with the presence of God. There was a cloud of glory over the Temple. This was similar to the cloud of glory over the Tabernacle in the wilderness with Moses. It means the presence of God is so strong that it changes what seems natural so that it glowing and radiant.

2 Chronicles 7: 7 And when Solomon finished praying, fire came down from the heavens and consumed the burnt offering and sacrifices, and the

glory of the Lord filled the temple. 2 And the priests were not able to enter into the house of the Lord, for the glory of the Lord filled the Lord's house. 3 And all the sons of Israel saw when the fire came down and the glory of the Lord came on the temple, and they bowed their faces low to the ground on the pavement, and they worshipped confessing,

5 EXPERIENCING THE GLORY

Experiencing the Glory

The people experienced the Spirit of God and it caused them to lie on the ground in worship. O don't know if you have been in a worship service where the presence of God is so strong that it causes the people to fall to the ground because of the glory. I have been in such services. All I wanted to do is worship and keep worshipping, Nothing else mattered in that place except God. I also know of other services where the glory of God is so strong people are healed or miracles occur because of the glory of God manifest in a specific place. The people there are worshipping and praising God but His presence is too overwhelming for our human bodies. Most people either lie on the floor or bow or kneel in a prostrate position because if the glory of God.

The people saw a visible expression of God's presence known as the Shekinah glory of God and it caused them to humble themselves in worship. Solomon's Temple was the first place that God said would be a permanent dwelling place for His Spirit. This is a covenant promise of God to the people of Israel. God promised Israel that He would have a temple in Jerusalem and that God's presence would be there. In the New Testament, Jesus informs us that He will return to Jerusalem to the Mt of Olives (Acts 1). He will reign on the earth in the temple [it must be rebuilt] for a thousand years before the white throne judgement.

Revelation 20: 4 I saw thrones, and they sat on them, and the authority to judge was given to them. And I saw the souls of those who had been beheaded for their witness of Jesus and for the word of God. They had not worshipped the beast or his image, and had not received his mark on their foreheads or on their hands. They came to life and reigned with Christ for a thousand years. 5 The rest of the dead did not come to life until the thousand years were ended. This is the first resurrection. 6 Blessed and holy is he who takes part in the first resurrection.

In the Presence of God

It can cause you to fall to the ground. People praise and worship.

Some see visions. Some prophesy. Some weep. Some pray quietly. This is not only in the old testament. When people gather to worship the LORD, they carry with them the presence of the LORD. The Holy Spirit who lives in us quickens our mortal bodies in such a way that overwhelms us.

As soon as you receive Christ, the Holy Spirit comes to live in you. In many churches the prayer of salvation is given to invite Jesus into your heart. Although it is true God comes to live on the inside of you, the term heart really means spirit. There is a glory on your life because God is living in you and through you.

John 20: 21 So Jesus said to them again, "Peace be with you. As My Father has sent Me, even so I send you." 22 When He had said this, He breathed on them and said to them, "Receive the Holy Spirit. 23 If you forgive the sins of anyone, they are forgiven them. If you retain the sins of anyone, they are retained."

More Glory

Once you are baptized in the Holy Spirit there is an overflow of the Holy Spirit. There is a stronger release of the glory of God on your life that will be evident to others. You will be a co labourer with Christ more. The more you press into God throughout your life, the more you will experience God using you and transforming you from glory to glory. God will use you to pray for others, to share Christ in what I would label divine connections. People will be in your life by no coincidence. The people in your life will need the very thing that you have. Those persons may ask you spiritual questions or simply need someone to speak encouragement to them God will use you. An example of this type of divine connection is the disciple Philip and the Ethiopian Eunuch. Philip was in a revival meeting of many people being saved and baptized with the Holy Spirit, but God specifically instructed him to go someplace else.

Acts 8: 26 Now an angel of the Lord said to Philip, "Rise up and go toward the south on the way that goes down from Jerusalem to Gaza." This is desert. 27 So he rose up and went. And there was a man of Ethiopia, a eunuch of great authority under Candace, queen of the Ethiopians, who was in command of her entire treasury. He had come to Jerusalem to worship. 28 He was returning, sitting in his chariot and reading the book of Isaiah the prophet. 29 The Spirit said to Philip, "Go to this chariot and stay with it."

As Philip obeys this instruction, there is an amazing result. The

Ethiopian Eunuch was reading the book of Isaiah and wanting to understand it. He could not understand it without help. Philip sat with him and preached Jesus Christ to him from the book of Isaiah and all the prophecies Jesus fulfilled as Messiah. The result was the Eunuch gave his life to Jesus Christ and desired to be water baptized. Not only did it change his life that day, but it brought the gospel to Africa. That person was in a position of authority. He could reach many people with the gospel.

Desire to be Baptized in the Holy Spirit

Jesus Himself is the Baptizer although often some person prays for you. It is a promise to all people who have accepted Christ. It empowers you for service so that you can effectively witness for Christ. There are gifts and there is evidence of God's supernatural presence as you lead others to Christ.

Acts 2: 38 Peter said to them, "Repent and be baptized, every one of you, in the name of Jesus Christ for the forgiveness of sins, and you shall receive the gift of the Holy Spirit. 39 For the promise is to you, and to your children, and to all who are far away, as many as the Lord our God will call."

The Baptism of the Holy Spirit releases such an overflow of the Spirit in your life that the gifts and manifestations of the Spirit begin to help you to win souls and build up the Church.

1 Corinthians 12: 4 There are various gifts, but the same Spirit. 5 There are differences of administrations, but the same Lord. 6 There are various operations, but it is the same God who operates all of them in all people. 7 But the manifestation of the Spirit is given to everyone for the common good. 8 To one is given by the Spirit the word of wisdom, to another the word of knowledge by the same Spirit, 9 to another faith by the same Spirit, to another gifts of healings by the same Spirit, 10 to another the working of miracles, to another prophecy, to another discerning of spirits, to another various kinds of tongues, and to another the interpretation of tongues. 11 But that one and very same Spirit works all these, dividing to each one individually as He will.
For a reason

The gifts listed above are not given for no reason. The gifts are given because they are necessary to effectively share Christ with others. The Holy Spirit's presence – God in us – gives us divine perspective concerning people and situations. For a complete teaching on the gifts of the Spirit, please refer to either my book on the gifts of the Holy Spirit or research the topic yourself. Benny Hinn is known for his excellent teaching on the person of the Holy Spirit and the presence of God.

For Private Worship

The baptism of the Holy Spirit gives us prayer language so we can effectively pray the will of God for us, through us. Really, the Holy Spirit gives us the words and the phrases and we pray them – coming into agreement with God as we pray in the Spirit and sing in the Spirit.

As we worship and pray in the Spirit and in our natural language together, God's presence is strong in us and we will feel promptings to do things or to help people or to give. Also, God may speak to us about ourselves. As we are communing, God's presence is strong in us and we are being transformed or changed. Each prayer encounter with God releases the glory of God in our lives in a particular way so that we are being changed from glory to glory. This can be compared to having a candle in a dark room – some light. More glory would mean someone turned on the light so there was no darkness remaining.

2 Corinthians 3 : 18 But we all, seeing the glory of the Lord with unveiled faces, as in a mirror, are being transformed into the same image from glory to glory by the Spirit of the Lord.

6 PASSION FOR GOD RELEASES GOD'S PRESENCE

Pray in the Prayer Language

If you are baptized in the Spirit thank God for it; Use the gift. Pray over yourself. I mean literally place hands on yourself and pray that God may use you in the gifts of the Spirit. Pray that God would give you divine connections. It is an awesome privilege being a partner with God. Once you start sharing Christ with others and seeing God miraculously flow through you to help others, you will want to do it more and more. You will have an eternal sense of destiny about your own life and want God to shine through you.

The Glory

The anointing is God's glory or God's presence living on the inside of you. It is your spirit, soul and body completely allowing God to use you. All your life long and throughout eternity God will be transforming us. There is no beginning or end to God. God is Omnipotent (all powerful) Omniscient (all knowing), Omnipresent (in all places). God is all wise. God is unconditional love. God is all merciful. God is beautiful beyond all beauty of the earth or the universe. God is more than any person could ever be. It is our intimate relationship with Him that transforms us.

The Glory of God is a Result not a Destiny

Never seek glory for yourself or because you want glory; that would be an impure motive. Glory is a result of our relationship with God. As we pray and serve God, the glory is evident. Remember always no matter what miracle The Holy Spirit might use you to do, God is the one who did it. God is the one who receives all the worship. You are a willing vessel – or a willing body. The term vessel is used in the King James Version and I like it because it is something that is ordinary and is used every day. Cups, glasses, jugs, pots are all vessels. They contain substances and can be reused daily. A person is like a vessel because God can fill us and use us for a particular task and the next day for something completely different.

Beauty

The beauty of creation is evidence of God's presence. The beauty of the earth and of all of the universes though is temporary.

Romans 1: 20 The invisible things about Him—His eternal power and deity—have been clearly seen since the creation of the world and are understood by the things that are made, so that they are without excuse.

The earth would have had a permanent beauty or glory of God as it did when it was first created by God with the first people: Adam and Eve. There would have been no death, no disease, no sickness, no wars, no hatred, no prejudice. People were created to be eternal. People would have never died. There was a glory about the garden of Eden. There were no thorns or thistles. It was lush and full of fruit and made as a perfect home for people. After sin entered the world, judgement came on Adam and Eve and all people who would be born after. Judgement came upon the earth itself. The effects of an obedience to God cannot be emphasized in any stronger way than showing this example. If they would have obeyed, our earth would be completely different.

Temporary

The most beautiful trees will lose their leaves and be as sticks during the winter. The most beautify animals will live a life span and die. Even the most beautiful woman or man, will show signs of aging. and eventually die- unless Jesus comes first. There are people who we choose as beauty queens or handsome men. Their bodies, their countenance is youthful, attractive and admirable. As they live on earth, 20 or 30 years, they do not stay the same. Oh, I have seen some people who take care of themselves so that at the age of 60 or 70, they are still attractive; they keep their body in shape and healthy and they can look good. I believe that as Christians we should do our best with the body God has given to us. We should care for our body so that we may live long and strong for God.

Let me give you an example of something I completely enjoy the beauty of– flowers. I am a gardener and I like to see flowers growing from bud to full flower. I enjoy them because it makes me feel closer to God`s creation. Tulips, geraniums, roses. They are so beautiful. Even the most beautiful orchid flower will fully bloom and then dry up. Yes, there could be new flowers, but that one flower has a life span. All of creation has a life span until Jesus comes.

Eternal

The beauty of God is eternal. It has no beginning and no end. It is constantly eternally radiant and fascinating. The glory of God will be revealed to us throughout all of eternity giving us pleasure as we learn more about him all of eternity. It is a hard concept to grasp for humans but we are going to live forever; living with God will be the most pleasure a person, a spirit, could possibly imagine.

As soon as you get a revelation of one aspect of God's beauty such as his mercy, a new revelation will come to you of his love. As you get a revelation of his love, you may realize He is Holy. As soon as one aspect of His glory is revealed to you, a different one will appear. I am saying throughout all of eternity we can be enjoying aspects of discovering new revelations of God. As we receive new revelation, we are being changed, transformed into Christ's image and likeness. Knowing God is experiential; the more you are in His presence, the more you are transformed.

Once you accept Jesus Christ as your Saviour, He lives on the inside of you. You are not perfect; you are a work in progress but God sees you are perfect because He sees the future as clearly as the present and the past. God is transforming you through His relationship with you. It is completely miraculous that the Omnipotent God of all of creation desires to live inside of humans and desires friendship with us. God wants to speak with us and lead us and comfort us and teach us.

2 Corinthians 4: 7 But we have this treasure in earthen vessels, the excellency of the power being from God and not from ourselves.

7 TRANSFORMED BY GLORY

The transformation is both outward and inward.

An example of a mighty transformation is the salvation of the Apostle Paul. As mentioned in Acts 9, Saul is on a journey to Damascus to oversee the arrest and killing of Christians. He was an enemy of the Christ. He was zealous for God but he believed killing Christians was God's will. He truly believed what he was doing was right. He was a Pharisee and very learned and wise. His passion meant he was willing to kill for God.

On that road to Damascus, a bright light appeared to him. It overwhelmed him. He heard a voice speak to him. Some people who were with them thought it was thunder. It was Jesus who spoke to him. As soon as he realized Jesus was speaking to him, he immediately repented of his old ways and offered himself to serve God.

Acts 9: 5 He said, "Who are You, Lord?"

The Lord said, "I am Jesus, whom you are persecuting. It is hard for you to kick against the goads." 6 Trembling and astonished, he said, "Lord, what will You have me do?" The Lord said to him, "Rise up and go into the city, and you will be told what you must do."

The Apostle Paul was blinded by the light. As he obeyed and went into the city to wait, Ananias was instructed by God to go pray for him. He was miraculously healed from blindness. He started preaching Jesus as Messiah in the very places he had once gone to arrest Christians. His transformation was so radical that the Jewish leaders who had once been his allies sought to kill him for blasphemy.

His life completely changed. His zeal was now to live for Christ. He wrote most of our New Testament. God used him to preach the gospel to the Gentiles, people who are not Jews. Rather than kill for God, he suffered a martyr's death and gave his life rather than deny his faith. The glory on his life was not because of his birth heritage or his education or any such thing. The glory on his life was because of God who lived in him and through him. The glory on your life is not because of you. It is because of Jesus Christ living in you and using you to share Christ, heal, deliver etc.

Transformed Lives

Before a person comes to Christ, he or she sins and lives a life that seems best to him or her. It is only by being born again by receiving Jesus as Saviour that we are given the chance for a godly holy life. Some outward things about your life will change. You won't go with the same crowd who liked to sin and enjoyed doing things against God or against the laws of your country. You will desire to be in the company of other Christians; you will want to learn more about God. Your life gets a new direction and priorities reflect your new life. Inwardly we are also transformed. Each decision you make to pursue God changes you. In God's presence, the joy overwhelms us. Revelations of His glory fascinates us. We become passionate about seeking Him more than anything.

The Presence of God

The presence of God in you or I as Christians is completely miraculous. God who is completely Holy comes to live in our earthly bodies inside of the human spirit. In the Old Testament, people couldn't even touch Mount Sinai or they would die while the glory of God was there as God spoke to Moses. That same Spirit of God that was evident in Exodus, that same Spirit of God that raised Jesus from the dead, lives inside of me and you if you are a Christian.

Romans 8: 11 But if the Spirit of Him who raised Jesus from the dead lives in you, He who raised Christ from the dead will also give life to your mortal bodies through His Spirit that lives in you.

Knowing that God`s presence is with us and our desire for His companionship will give us lives of joy, pleasure, fulfillment and divine connections. It is almost like living in heaven on earth. You must cultivate your relationship with God to experience it. It includes a life of prayer, worship, praise, giving, serving, obedience, desiring and obeying God`s Word, the company of other Christians that sharpen us and compliment us. If we truly live for God with all our being, God will manifest Himself in our lives.

Deuteronomy 11: 20 You shall write them on the doorposts of your house and on your gates, 21 so that your days and the days of your children may be multiplied in the land which the Lord swore to your fathers to give them, as long as the days of heaven on the earth.

As you read the Word of God and as you pray and pursue God, His presence is upon your life in a special way. The glory of God is on your life because God is living in you and through you. His presence is the glory. His Holy Spirit filling the human spirit causes the glory to be seen. It is a witness to those who are not Christians. We will desire to do God's will and obey His promptings and leadings. As you obey God's direction to speak with people, or to give or to pray, the evidence will show you are a Christian. Your giving and serving others and showing love and mercy to others, reveals God's glory to those who do not yet know God. It will cause them to want to know why you are doing those things. It may get them curious enough to seek God and become Christians.

Matthew 5: 16 Let your light so shine before men that they may see your good works and glorify your Father who is in heaven.

God uses Humans who are Willing and Obedient

The person who lead me to the LORD was being used by God is in a mighty way. As he was speaking, I saw a radiance on him. It was almost as though he was an angel. He was prophesying over me, using the gifts of discerning of spirits, words of wisdom and words of knowledge. He was saying things that I knew only God and I knew about. Secret things I had only shared with God, this earthen vessel was speaking. There was a glow or a radiance about him. I knew that I knew God was using him to speak to me. God was using him to communicate with me. It was such a strong witness to me that I immediately prayed – repentance and accepting Jesus Christ as Saviour and LORD.

Even afterwards, he and his wife and family invested in me bringing me to church and talking with me. I had to realize that it was God's glory on him and that he was truly human. It was hard for me to realize that he was a human because God had used him so mightily to speak to me the day of my salvation. His appearance was radiant and the words he spoke revealed the most secret parts of my heart that only God knew. It was although God had to keep reminding me that he was only a man but he was a man willing to be used by God. Our obedience to God can lead people to Christ. Our willingness to be used, makes us vessels of the glory. God can pour through us to affect the lives of others. It can have eternal consequences.

We cannot worship the vessels or the people who share Christ with us. We should respect and honour them yes, but we should not worship them. We don't worship the pastors or apostles or prophets or evangelists or teachers. God uses them; we should respect them. Only God is worthy to be worshipped. He chooses to use us, mere humans to work with Him or to help Him impact the lives of people throughout our lives on earth. I would describe this as pouring liquid from a tea pot into a cup or mug. The mug isn't the best part of the tea. It is the liquid inside that gives us a delightful drink. God pours His glory in us and through us to reach those who need God.

If God uses someone to encourage you or prophesy over you or teach you etc. give glory to God. Thank God for sending you help. Thank God for answering your prayer. Pray for the person that God would bless him or her and continue to use him or her so more people could be saved, healed, delivered etc. pray that God will use you as well. As someone has taught you, so you should also teach others. What you have received, you should also give to others.

Matthew 10: 7 As you go, preach, saying, 'The kingdom of heaven is at hand.' 8 Heal the sick, cleanse the lepers, raise the dead, and cast out demons. Freely you have received, freely give.

The more you know God the more you will grow in discerning of spirits and the other gifts of the spirit. You can literally see the glory of God on a person. You see it with your spirit. There is a glow or radiance upon the person. The Holy Spirit becomes so strong on a person with the anointing that you can see the person as a messenger from God. The person's words will impact your life directly – right into your spirit. The person's countenance or appearance is beautiful, radiant. You realize it is God using the person who is preaching or teaching or ministering in some way.

8 THE ANOINTING RELEASES
THE GIFTS OF GOD

The Anointing

The anointing is God's presence evident in a person because of the effectiveness of his or her ministry. The words or the actions have spiritual significance. You see it with your spirit. The person will be using the gifts of the Holy Spirit, tongues, interpretation, discerning of spirits, prophesy, words of wisdom, words of knowledge, gifts of healings, gift of faith, working of miracles, the gift of serving the gift of giving, the gift of teaching, the gift of encouragement, the gift of leadership, the gift of mercy. Please research each of these gifts if you do not know what they are. [I discuss them in the Book on Spiritual Gifts].

The gifts come strong because of the presence of God. The glory of God brings a release of the giftings of God. Even people who are not saved can see a glow about a person filled to overflowing with God's Spirit, but they will not understand it. Should you see the glory of God on a person or on yourself, thank God for using that person. You worship God and offer yourself as a vessel God can use.

Shekinah Glory

Some people believe the Shekinah glory of God was only in the Old Testament. The presence of God in the ark of the covenant. This treasure in an earthen vessel is the LORD Jesus Christ living on the inside of you. It is God filling you with His presence to accomplish righteousness on the earth. It isn't so we can have goose bumps or a special feeling. Oh yes. These feelings might occur, but the reason God fills us is so that He can use us on earth to do the will of God.

There could be someone praying. You may be the answer to their prayer. The words you speak could encourage a person, release faith or be the catalyst for a miracle. You could be used to quote a scripture to touch someone bringing healing. God uses earthen vessels. He can use angels. Sometimes He does but mostly He likes to use people – people who willingly give themselves to God who give God all the glory. The anointing of the LORD is always for a purpose. It is to transform us but also to make us a minister of His mercy: salvation, healing, deliverance.

Isaiah 61: 1 The Spirit of the Lord God is upon me
   because the Lord has anointed me
   to preach good news to the poor;
He has sent me to heal the broken-hearted,
   to proclaim liberty to the captives,
    and the opening of the prison to those who are bound;
2 to proclaim the acceptable year of the Lord
   and the day of vengeance of our God;
to comfort all who mourn,
3   to preserve those who mourn in Zion,
to give to them beauty
   for ashes,
the oil of joy
   for mourning,
the garment of praise
   for the spirit of heaviness,
that they might be called trees of righteousness,
   the planting of the Lord,
   that He might be glorified.

As you read the passage above realize it is a Messianic prophecy that Jesus Christ fulfilled while He was on earth. Please also recognize that you are a member of the body of Christ on the earth today and this is your mandate. This sacred vision is for you. Read it and pray it identifying with Jesus. Pray it over yourself. God didn't save you and baptize you in the Holy Spirit for no reason. God wants to use you as a member of the body of Christ. The anointing is for the mission of sharing the good news of Jesus as Saviour, Healer, Deliverer with all people from all nations.

In some secular jobs, you can't openly preach Christ, but you can with excellence give your best efforts so they shine with the glory of God. You can with diligence and wisdom, serve and show special care for each person you meet. It will cause them to want to know the reason for your joy. You may pray for them. You might be the only Christian who does. Your life can cause them to want to know God.

Christian, stir up your spiritual gifts. Lay hands on yourself and pray "I stir up the gifts of the Spirit". Literally pray that God would use you and expect Him to do it. Pray in tongues and pray in your natural language. Build yourself up in the Holy faith so that God may use you. Realize that the day you became a Christian was the start of an awesome life with God. God wants to use you. Are you willing? Would you say yes to God using you? You must be willing and you must be obedient. You believe in Christ, you are a disciple.

This word to go preach the gospel is for all of the Church. I would say point at your own self right now and read these words. They are God's will for your life; you are a Christian, you are on earth for a purpose. The purpose is more than your career or your family although it certainly includes them. God's will is for you to share the gospel – the good news that you accepted and have received. The presence of God in you quickens you so that you can. It is the anointing of God that empowers you to be a living witness of God living in an earthen vessel that others might come to know Him.

Mark 16: 15 He said to them, "Go into all the world, and preach the gospel to every creature. 16 He who believes and is baptized will be saved. But he who does not believe will be condemned. 17 These signs will accompany those who believe: In My name, they will cast out demons; they will speak with new tongues; 18 they will take up serpents; if they drink any deadly thing, it will not hurt them; they will lay hands on the sick, and they will recover."

Acts 1: 8 But you shall receive power when the Holy Spirit comes upon you. And you shall be My witnesses in Jerusalem, and in all Judea and Samaria, and to the ends of the earth."

May you who want to know about the anointing, read this book and claim it for your own life. I pray you will realize Jesus saved you for a purpose. Yes, salvation is so we can go to heaven but it is also so we can live on earth in victory and win others to Christ. The Holy Spirit, the Holy presence is the glory of God. They are inseparable. There cannot be an anointing without the presence of God and vice versa. It cannot be faked. It cannot be bought. It cannot be manufactured. God manifests His presence as we desire Him more than anything else. It is the Spirit of the living God living in you, on you and through you so that you might be a co labourer with God: to save, to heal, to deliver, to preach good news.

9 THE LIVING WATER

Living Water

Ezekiel 47: 1 Then he brought me back to the door of the temple; and water was flowing out from under the threshold of the temple eastward, for the front of the temple faced east; the water was flowing down from under from the right side of the temple, south of the altar. 2 Then he brought me out by way of the north gate, and led me around on the outside to the outer gate that faces east; and the water was coming out on the south side.

3 When the man who had the line in his hand went eastward, he measured a thousand cubits, and he brought me through the water; the water reached the ankles. 4 Again he measured a thousand and brought me through the water. The water reached the knees. Again he measured a thousand and brought me through the water. The water reached the loins. 5 Afterward he measured a thousand. And it was a river that I could not pass over, for the water had risen, enough water to swim in, a river that could not be passed over. 6 He said to me, "Son of man, have you seen this?"

Then he brought me and caused me to return to the brink of the river. 7 When I had returned I saw on the bank of the river very many trees on the one side and on the other. 8 Then he said to me, "This water flows toward the eastern region and goes down into the valley, and enters the sea. When it flows into the sea, the water will become fresh. 9 Every living creature that swarms, wherever the rivers go, will live. And there shall be a very great multitude of fish, because these waters shall come there and the others become fresh. Thus, everything shall live wherever the river comes. 10 It shall come to pass that the fishermen shall stand upon it. From En Gedi even to En Eglaim there shall be a place to spread out nets. Their fish shall be according to their kinds, as the fish of the Mediterranean Sea, exceedingly many. 11 But its miry places and its marshes shall not be healed. They shall be given to salt. 12 By the river upon its bank, on this side and on that side, shall grow all kinds of trees for food, whose leaf shall not fade nor shall its fruit fail. They shall bring forth fruit according to their months, because their water issues out of the sanctuary. And their fruit shall be for food and their leaves for medicine."

The Holy Spirit

Imagine this scene. A huge chocolate cake with chocolate frosting is brought to you. It is your birthday. Chocolate is your favourite. You get a large piece. You want another one. You like it because it is your favourite and because its your birthday you indulge. Kids though, would not stop at a second piece. They may choose to eat the cake instead of their dinner. If you asked them how much they wanted it – they would show you by how they consumed it.

I want to describe Ezekiel's vision by asking the question: How much of God do you want? Nothing can stop you from desiring more of God. Nothing can stop you from pursuing God with passion. The only hindrance to you not growing in God is your own self. If you do not want more of God, God will never force you to come to Him. Salvation is a choice. You choose to accept Jesus as Saviour.

Serving God is a choice you make each day, moment by moment. It originates with the human will – the part that is a unique living soul that God created to shine His glory through.
God will speak to you, lead you, prompt you and encourage you. God will nudge you, remind you of someone to pray for or of someone to minister to – but never will He force you to serve Him. It is a choice we must make as we live our lives.

Ankle Depth

The scripture above is Ezekiel's vision of the river of the Holy Spirit that flows from the throne of God. This river is described as starting from the Throne of God and is so plentiful that it causes trees to spring up on both sides of it. When they first entered the river, it was at 1000 cubits. The water was to the ankle. (A cubit is approximately 21 inches).

You can have as much of God as you want. The Holy Spirit lives in you and will teach you, lead you into all truth, guide you, remind you of what God has taught you in the past. The Holy Spirit comforts you, teaches and instructs you, brings revelation to you. As you press in to seek God, how much do you want? Do you want a short thank you God? That is how I would describe water at the ankles. You can roll up your pant legs and walk in ankle deep water. You are passing through with no desire to stay. It is a refreshing, dip in the water.

This person who walks with God at ankle depth, is living his or her life as a Christian. You received Jesus as Saviour. Probably you attend a church. Mostly though, you are doing things on your own. You are living your life with most of your being in the present world system. Perhaps its entertainment or hobbies or sports; you are doing things that are good, nothing wrong but you are not pursuing God with passion.

This ankle depth person is saved, enjoying life with some spiritual input from God. To the people in the world, this person is almost the same except for the Jesus issue. This person will see God as an important part of his or her life. That person sees God as only one component part of his or her whole life. It is a shallow level of Christianity but I'm not saying they might not get to heaven. Jesus blood is the only way to get to heaven. On the earth, though, while this person could have been used by God to share Christ, pray for people, win souls, etc. God could have, would have had such a more fulfilling life for that person.

Knee Deep

Next, Ezekiel walked in 1000 more cubits and came in to the knee depth of the water. Please know this person has either got to be wearing shorts or is going to have wet pants. To go knee deep into water is making more of a commitment. This person may be going to a church and perhaps attending more than one service a week. This person may be doing some type of devotional each day. This person doesn't want to go swimming. This person is walking through the water. Most of his or her body is above the water. He or she can move his hands or feet. He or she may be in there to take pictures of their children or of the scenery. This person is not staying in the water very long.

I can remember once my sister and her husband took me to the beach. We went to the closest one. I was perhaps 2 or 3 years old. As I walked into the water with my sister, I could walk and walk and walk and it didn't get any deeper than my waist. The water was at my sister's knee level. Although I loved it and wanted to stay, my sister was not staying because she couldn't swim in the water. It was too shallow for her. We travelled further and went to a beach that she could swim in. When you want to go swimming, you don't want knee level water.

Waist Deep

Once more he measured 1000 cubits. It was at the waist level. Waist level is the comfort level for people who can't swim. Half of the person's body is above water and the lower part under water. My mom liked to go at waist level. She didn't like deep water. She could swim but didn't like water that she couldn't walk out of. She didn't have to swim. She could still walk around and be cool in the water but it wasn't deep enough to make her swim.

This is a place of further commitment. You are giving yourself more to God. This person would probably read the Bible and do a devotional. This person would probably attend church faithfully. This person may share his or her testimony with someone should the Holy Spirit lead him or her. This person is committed to God, but he or she is not getting the benefits of the depths of God. Compare it to your gas gauge.

If your car gas gauge is at ½ do you stop and buy gas or are you the type of person who lets it go until it is on empty? My dad used to pride himself on running on empty. The light would be flashing on empty and my dad would smile and say " I can get it to go further." We would beg him to stop and get gas. He wouldn't. I am talking about on a long trip from Ontario to British Columbia. We were in the car and we were so nervous. Most of the time he could coast into the gas station and get gas. Ah, but there was the instance in risk taking that made him have to walk on the highway to a gas station because of his stubborn pride. None of us laughed at him. All of us were glad that he made it there and back.

A Christian with half of his or her life committed to God can be used by God. This person may be refreshed by church services and prayer. This person is sort of in between the two worlds of heaven and earth. What I mean by that is this person knows God – but there are other things more important half of his or her day or life. The danger of staying at this level is that when waves get stronger or winds blow, the person may be trying to live on empty.

The River that could not be passed over

Finally, the scripture talks about the next 1000 cubits where there is a river that could not be passed over. The water is so deep. The person must swim. Almost all of the body is in the water. Even your head gets wet. Your face gets wet. You have to know how to breathe to stay in that level of water. A person who can swim and who likes to swim chooses this level of water.

I remember myself as an elementary school child. My sister would take me to a special pool near her house. A life guard was there. I mostly stayed in the first half of the pool. I could walk into the water to my waist level. I knew that marker was to mark the deep end. I knew the water would be over my head. My sister taught me to swim. I could float and kick my feet and move my arms. I could swim under water. I could dog paddle. I knew I could swim.

One day at that pool, I met a friend who could swim. She came into the shallow side with me but wasn't happy to stay there. She wanted to dive from the diving board in the deep end. She convinced me that if I could swim in the shallow end, I could surely swim in the deep end. I believed her. It was a big step for me that day. I got into line with the other kids who were waiting for the diving board. I always wanted to go off the diving board. As it was my turn, I planned my course. I would dive directly in the direction of the deep end ladder. I knew I could swim under water because I could swim the width of the pool under water. I dove off into the deep water and my body did its normal swimming. Within seconds I was at the ladder. It boosted my confidence as a swimmer. I relaxed and swam in the deep end from that day on.

A person who plunges into the depths of God will not seem normal to the people who are not Christians. This person is radical. I mean radically sold out for God. This person believes the reason for his or her life is to live for God and to bring God glory. This person may go to church more than one service. This person may serve in the church. This person may witness to people in the workplace or in his or her leisure life. This person desires God's Word more than anything. This person will read God's word over and over. This person will do devotionals plus.

This person realizes that God's Word, The Holy Bible, is a direct statement from God to us His people. This person will pray because he or she knows God answers prayer yes. This person will also take pleasure in worship and prayer knowing that God loves him or her. This person considers the Holy Spirit first. Pastor Yonggi Chou from Korea (church of over 100, 000 members) has a book titled The Holy Spirit: My Senior Partner. In the book, he describes living for God with every moment of every day. He prays about 6 hours a day. Their church is known for its radical dedication to prayer and service for Christ. They go on a mountain prayer mountain for days of fasting and prayer. God is the reason we live. We live not only to commune with God but to share Christ with others. Constantly this person is in prayer and intercession and praise.

International House of Prayer

A North American example of the praying Church in Korea can be seen in International House of Prayer Kansas City. The people are in prayer 24 hours a day, 7 days a week. They have more than one prayer room with somebody praising, praying and worshipping constantly. Yes. There is a local congregation. Not everyone who attends is a full time missionary intercessor but some are. They worship God and are given in prayer and service to God more than 6 hours a day. This prayer movement began in 1999 as a full time intercessory body. God has blessed and prospered them. Materials from that church are sent out in other languages. People from other nations come there to pray and seek God. They are world famous for their conferences that teach on prayer and a life given wholly to God. They are praying to build churches and International Houses of prayer all over the earth.

God is the most important aspect of life. Those who plunge into the rivers of God over their heads are giving all of themselves, to God. They will be used by God to evangelize, to heal the sick, to deliver those in addictions. They will press into God and radiate the glory of God in their being. They live for Christ. The stuff of earth is joyful and they thank God for it, such as families, jobs, sports etc. They will always keep choosing God first. Their families will be radical for God. Their homes will be places of refreshing and their relationship with God will be stronger privately than even their membership or belonging in a church. God is the first. God can use such men and women to intercede for mercy for our nations. God can use such people to be Apostles, Prophets, Evangelists, Teachers and Pastors. God will use them in serving and in giving and in living lives of excellence that shine the light of Christ.

Waters to Swim in

Please do not think this teaching is to condemn you if you relate to the ankle deep, knee deep or waist deep levels of knowing God; it is only meant to show you there is more. A married person must care for his or her spouse. Parents must care for their children. People are comfortable at different levels of commitment with God. You can have as much of God as you want. Some people choose a family. Some people choose sports. Some people choose the arts. They can swim in the depths and then go back to their waist level of living. Usually, during special conferences or during revival meetings, the Holy Spirit flows so strong that people are fixed on God more than anything else – they go deep.

I speak as one who knows what it is like to know the pleasure of God sharing His heart with me. I know the mercy He has shown me. I know the love and holiness of His presence and know how radically He saved me from the uttermost. God called me unto Himself although there was no Christian in my family. God saved me. God called me to Himself so that I have continued to press in more and more throughout the past thirty something years of my life. I choose God. I so thank God for the freedoms of living in Canada where I can freely worship God without persecution. In other countries, people die for their faith. I can choose to praise and worship God with all my being living my life as a worshipper and as an intercessor. God can use me because I am His. It means being willing and obedient. It means constant communion with God, praying without ceasing.

God can give you the measure you want. You can choose. It is your choice. How much do you want? God has more for you than you have ever known. God can reveal His will to you as you commune with Him. He can talk to you as friend with friend. God can use you to minister. That is if you are married or you are single. If you are single, give all your life to Christ. Get as much of God as you can. Teenagers have only several commitments and much free time. They could be playing video games with their friends. They could be doing sports. They could be praying for people and seeing them healed. They could be evangelizing their sports teams. They could be serving and giving within the local church. I truly believe that youth, teens, twenty somethings, thirty somethings with a desire for God first cannot be stopped. I believe they could seriously make the commission to preach Christ in all the earth possible because of their total surrender to God.

Into the Depths of God

You are praising and praying most of your life. You will be worshipping throughout the day, praying throughout the day. I had this experience and I didn't know others also had it. I would wake up with my spirit singing with the Holy Spirit within me. The song would be in my spirit. I believe God was singing in me and through me. I had a teacher who also shared this experience with our class, so I realized other people can also have it. God`s worship and praise rolling around in your spirit throughout the day and throughout the night – its like living in heaven on earth. Your spirit (being) is the part of you that God has connection with.

If I took this same example and asked you how much money do you want, most people would want all they could get. There is a priority on wealth in our culture. Money is the prime concern of may people. Even rich people if asked how much money they want would answer more please. If you were walking ankle deep in hundred dollar bills would you be content to stay there? You can have all the money around you. Would you want to stay at knee level? Would you be satisfied at the waist level? I don't believe there is anyone in North America who would stay at the ankle level. I believe most people would try to cover their heads with money, except they would ask for a straw so they could breath. Most people want all the money they can get.

No one in North American culture or Western Society would consider it strange to want more money. We could be so passionate about money, but are we that passionate about God? Wanting God though could cause them to be cautious. Worldly people cannot understand. Some Christians won`t understand. The flesh in them doesn't want to die. You cannot keep wanting more of God, giving yourself wholly to God without the flesh dying. Pursuing life in the Spirit is beyond all earthly pleasure.

Galatians 5: 24 Those who are Christ's have crucified the flesh with its passions and lusts. 25 If we live in the Spirit, let us also walk in the Spirit.

There are dimensions of the Holy Spirit; this includes the baptism of the Holy Spirit. There are depths to the glory of Christ; there are multi dimensions to the Word of God. Knowing God is an unending pleasure as He revels more of His glory to us.

Rivers to Swim in

Some years ago, I was in a strong prophetic meeting awaiting the laying on of hands and prophesy. The Spirit of God was so strong in the atmosphere, my legs trembled. Suddenly out of my innermost being a prophetic word came forth: "Rivers to swim in. There are rivers to swim in. Don't stay by the side of the river or in the shallow places but go in all the way – rivers to swim in." I roared like a lion. I knew it wasn't me. The Holy Spirit spoke through me strongly. After wards prophecies began to be released all throughout the room. I could feel God speaking to me in my spirit. I had to sit down because my legs were trembling so much. I felt the presence of God so strong it was as though I were seeing it from the point of view of sitting with Christ on the Throne viewing my earthly body and soul living on earth. The presence of God was so strong, it lasted several hours and the only thing I can say is I wish I would have praised more, worshipped more, prayed more, listened more.

I knew that through the prophetic word, God was referring to the passage of scripture about levels of knowing Him in the Holy Spirit as the levels of water in Ezekiel. I knew God was speaking to me, but also knew it wasn't only for me but also for those in the room. I believe the word is also for you, dear reader of this message, as I believe God gives me revelation of Him to share with others that you might know Him more intimately.

Giving your all to God or swimming in the depths of the Holy Spirit means you are going forward. You are moving in a direction. You are not caught up with trivial things. The Word of God will seem to be very important to you. God will speak to you and you will treasure the words knowing they are for you. In this place of yielding to the Holy Spirit, yes you will be attending church services. Yes, you will be reading God's Word and studying it but you will also be meditating on it and confessing it. You will be involved in ministry in your church but also in evangelizing. Your life will be lived from a divine perspective.

You will know that your life on earth is only temporary. You will view life from the point of view of you seated on the throne with Christ. Things of the earth are not unimportant but they viewed with a sober eternal perspective. You realize the greatness of God. You realize you are more than a conqueror through Christ and that through Him you can do all things. You are ready for assignments that God will give you because you are praying and worshipping and communing with God.

People with passion for God, may sneak their Bibles into their secular workplace so they can read portions of God's Word during their coffee breaks. They will be praying for people throughout their ordinary day as though it really mattered, because it does. These people will pray over the Word of God as they receive it saying "O God make this word a part of my life. I receive this word for me. Let it be mixed with faith producing in me life and health and peace, praying, God can give me 100-fold increase of this Word in my life. The 100-fold increase is a maximum harvest". Jesus referred to the Word of God as precious seed sown into people's lives that brings forth a harvest (Mark 4: 20).

People who are living in the Spirit like to live in the Spirit. People who are living in the Spirit, will pray asking God to help them with ordinary tasks knowing that God's blessing on them will give them excellence beyond what all human education and skill can produce. I mean this for the work place, for dinners, for business activities, for leisure activities, walking, jogging, playing sports, at home or at the movies or with a group of friends. These people realize everywhere they go they carry Christ with them. These people speak to God (inwardly) all though out the day. These people will want to commune with God knowing that it is God who can help them to do excellently beyond all education and training.

Christians living in the Spirit will be friends with Christians who love God the way they do. Their friends will be as scripture says as iron sharpening iron (Proverbs 27: 17). They will encourage each other and complement each other to excellence and brilliance. The friends together will be stronger than the sum of their parts. They will have words of encouragement between them that strengthen both of them.

Matthew 18: 19 "Again I say to you, that if two of you agree on earth about anything they ask, it will be done for them by My Father who is in heaven. 20 For where two or three are assembled in My name, there I am in their midst."

The dynamic presence of God in the midst of Christian families or Christian friendships is a strength beyond all other types of strength. This is for sure true in prayer but also in sharing together and in getting together whether it be to go to a movie, to play a sport or to talk about God. People living in the Spirit draw strength from God; living in the Holy Spirit is what gives us insight, revelation, wisdom etc.

In The Depths With God

Start your day by praising and worshipping. Commit yourself to God each day. Pray that God will use you throughout the day. I like to start the day with prayer and praise. If it is not possible, pray at the end of the day. Throughout the day, ask God to use you. If you are living in the Spirit, focused on Christ, God can and will use you. There are opportunities God will bring your way to intercede and to witness to people. I would like to compare it to this: field agents. There are companies that have field agents, people who are on call that will come and repair your plumbing or your roof or whatever. They are field agents. They go to a job, ready to receive an opportunity for new assignments. They complete the job and afterwards they go to the next one. As Christians, we should be field agents for God. If we are in communion with Him, and we are led by the Holy Spirit, we can make a difference in people's lives. Kind words, serving, giving are ways we can impact people's lives. You can be a field agent of righteousness. You can obey the promptings of the Holy Spirit and shine the light of Christ in the earth.

God could impress upon you to speak a kind word to a person making his or her day. God can use you to help someone you don't even know so that he or she would know God cares. What if God could trust you with the treasures of Heaven to give to the people on the earth? You would have to be serving and giving in obedience to the Holy Spirit's promptings. You may be in an ordinary place such as a supermarket or mall, God may move you inwardly to speak to a stranger. God may use you to bless someone. What if you had more than enough money that week? Someone in the line in front of you didn't have enough money to buy all that was on the conveyer belt. He or she would start removing items. You could step in and say – I'd be glad to pay for that. God has blessed me. Please receive it as a gift from God. You could use your giving to be a witness to that person.

You may see a person in a crowd but off to the side, crying alone. You could offer to pray for that person. God can use you to bring peace or healing to that person. Our obedience to the promptings of the Holy Spirit can glorify God. Pray that you could be a person God could trust with the secret things – things that involve eternal significance like souls. You don't have to give the steps to salvation to reach someone for God. Your first dealings with someone can soften his or her heart to receiving Jesus as Saviour.

The Body of Christ

You can be the hands of Christ by serving and giving. You can help someone carry packages. You may speak only a few words to someone, but be bringing the exact words that person needs to hear. There are so many people in places of business and commerce. Not too many are looking for opportunities to be a blessing to someone else. Your mouth should be speaking things that are true, positive, kind, bringing peace, bringing comfort. You may speak a scripture or paraphrase a scripture. You should be speaking words that sow life into people: words that encourage, comfort, build up, strengthen.

Philippians 4: 8 Finally, brothers, whatever things are true, whatever things are honest, whatever things are just, whatever things are pure, whatever things are lovely, whatever things are of good report, if there is any virtue, and if there is any praise, think on these things.

To be a field agent of God's righteousness, you 've got to give yourself wholly to Him. As you pursue God, you will become immersed in His presence. You've got to want God more than you want anything. The closer your relationship with God, the more you will want to help people.

You realize the only hope for people is Jesus. The truth is loving God manifest itself through Christ likeness: loving people. Be willing to love God with all your being. You will have the most exciting life possible. You could be a tree of righteousness planted by living waters (Is 61:3). God can prosper you above and beyond what you make in your salary. God prospers you because it is His pleasure but also so you can be a giver. You can give money to the gospel – to ministers who bring the gospel to the nations. You can help people by giving finances or things they have need of. God can prosper you so that you could make a difference by your giving.

Matthew 22: 37 Jesus said to him, "'You shall love the Lord your God with all your heart, and with all your soul, and with all your mind.'[c] 38 This is the first and great commandment. 39 And the second is like it: 'You shall love your neighbor as yourself.'[d] 40 On these two commandments hang all the Law and the Prophets."

Education and Training

We can reach people for God through our jobs and our schools and by connecting with all people in our lives. God wants to use your education and training and skills to help others. This is in your career but also as a servant ministry. If you do not have a job, pray that God would give you a job. Pray that you could get your education and training. The more qualifications you have, the more opportunities there are for God to use you in different ways. I highly encourage you to get as much education and training as possible. This is something people might consider being earthly minded but the truth is it gives you the credentials to be in a place, a position, so that you can encounter people there and be a light for Christ. Being a light includes living with integrity and wholeheartedness. It includes doing your best in your job or your volunteer work with excellence. It includes going over and above what is expected of you. God wants people in all spheres of society.

In 1995, Bill Bright (Campus Crusade) and Loren Cunningham (Youth with a Mission) identified 7 spheres of authority that people have on the earth. They are as follows:

Education
Economy
Media
Government
Family
Religion/Church

Entertainment

I would add in the spheres of health care and technology because these are important fields of influence. Each of us has several areas of influence. If you are a student, you have influence in your school, your job, your home, the church etc. Please see that each person is unique. You may reach people I never meet and vice versa. The point is that the Body of Christ in the earth, should influence every area of society. I believe it is God's desire to have Christians over flowing with the presence of God in all areas of life on earth. There should be no area where there is not Christian influence. You should know your areas of influence and pray for God to use you in them – I mean specifically name them to God praying for wisdom and leading. The goal is to bring this gospel of the kingdom throughout all the earth, to all nations, to all people groups. The Body of Christ is called corporately to go preach Christ or to send others but also to shine the light of Christ in your spheres of influence.

Christians Should Shine

Godly character, kindness, mercy, integrity, wisdom, caring, serving, giving, these are aspects of life that Christians should shine in. They are character qualities of Christ. In our earth these qualities show a difference than the mass of people who live in darkness not knowing Christ. If you are in the news, much of it is negative; therefore, give a good report – something positive. If you are in entertainment, much of it is impure; therefore, be holy and set apart for God. If you are in education, not many give credit to God; therefore, be humble and thankful. If you are in government, many are corrupt; therefore, be honest and genuine. If you are in the economics, field, many are negative; therefore, be positive and prayerful and offer alternatives. In the field of family, many are selfish; therefore, consider your family members and care for them as much as you love yourself. In the field of health care, many are negative; therefore, use God's standard as the hope for healing. In the field of technology, man's wisdom is emphasized as most important; therefore, rely on God who knows all things and can give you wisdom above all earthly wisdom.

God can use you with your talents, gifts and education.

Proverbs 18: 16 A man's gift makes room for him,
    and brings him before great men.

You Should be Passionate for Jesus

If you do not feel your first love for God, passionate desire for God, repent and ask God to renew you. Thank God for saving your soul and baptizing you in the Holy Spirit. Begin to thank God for what he has done for you. Rededicate yourself to God. Pray that He would lead you in your relationships, your spheres of authority. Pray and stir yourself up in the Holy Spirit. Literally pray "I stir myself up in the Holy Spirit that Christ might be glorified."

Jesus promised there would be a wellspring of God inside of you.

A well spring never runs dry. It bubbles up out of the ground and sometimes becomes a river.

John 4: 10 Jesus answered her, "If you knew the gift of God, and who it is who is saying to you, 'Give Me a drink,' you would have asked Him, and He would have given you living water."

13 Jesus said to her, "Everyone who drinks of this water will thirst again, 14 but whoever drinks of the water that I shall give him will never thirst. Indeed, the water that I shall give him will become in him a well of water springing up into eternal life."

Christians are meant to live in a place of overflow of the presence of God. The living water or Holy Spirit of God should bubble forth from the spirit. If there are hindrances to the flowing of joy and the life of Christ in our lives, we must pray that God will quicken them to us so that we may by prayer and action remove them. A supernatural joy should be springing up from within a Christian daily. We should be joyful and overflowing with the love of Christ.

You received eternal life the day you accepted Jesus Christ as your Saviour. You don't get eternal life when you die; you get it as soon as you receive Christ. Although we live on the earth, we are not of the earth. We live in the Spirit while we are living on the earth: we live in the Spirit although we have physical bodies. God will give us vision to see things from His vantage point. God can give us inside wisdom, discerning beyond all earthly knowledge. Yes, God wants to use your education and training but especially because you are a spirit being, flowing with the Holy Spirit.

John 7: 37 On the last and greatest day of the feast, Jesus stood and cried out, "If anyone is thirsty, let him come to Me and drink. 38 He who believes in Me, as the Scripture has said, out of his heart shall flow rivers of living water." 39 By this He spoke of the Spirit, whom those who believe in Him would receive. For the Holy Spirit was not yet given, because Jesus was not yet glorified

Once more Jesus refers to the Holy Spirit as living water. Once more He describes it as an eternal well flowing from out of the heart or core of being. God is the source of supply. Again, in Revelation God uses the analogy of the Holy Spirit as a river of life. This is in the New Jerusalem, the new heavens and new earth. The life giving Holy Spirit is emphasized.

Revelation 22: 1 Then he showed me a pure river of the water of life, clear as crystal, flowing from the throne of God and of the Lamb 2 in the middle of its street. On each side of the river was the tree of life, which bore twelve kinds of fruit, yielding its fruit each month. The leaves of the tree were for the healing of the nations. 3 There shall be no more curse. The throne of God and of the Lamb shall be in it, and His servants shall serve Him. 4 They shall see His face, and His name shall be on their foreheads. 5 Night shall be no more. They need no lamp nor the light of the sun, for the Lord God will give them light. And they shall reign forever and ever.

This chapter is almost a mirror image of the chapter in Ezekiel including the trees planted by the sides of it. Ezekiel had the same vision as the apostle John of the river of life. This image is present as we draw our strength from God now, but it is also to come – a new heavens and earth created by God with a New Jerusalem where the Lamb of God will be the light of it.

Right after Jesus saying that He is coming soon, these words appear:

Revelation 22: 17 The Spirit and the bride say, "Come." Let him who hears say, "Come." Let him who is thirsty come. Let him who desires take the water of life freely.

This scripture speaks prophetically of what is to occur on the earth. The Church (The Body of Christ all over the earth) will be crying out "Come. Come Lord Jesus." The whole Church will be singing praise for the LORD to return. We will be moved with prayer and invitation for Christ to return. There will be a move of the Holy Spirit in the earth wooing men and women and children to want the LORD's return. Both the Holy Spirit and the human spirit will agree on the need for the coming of Jesus. People will want God's return. The promise Jesus made to us is that He would return and come rule and reign on the earth. It has been over 2, 000 years but the promise has not yet been fulfilled. I believe the reason God has not yet come is that God is so merciful, He is giving people a chance to repent. There are billions of people on the planet that have not yet had opportunity to hear the good news of Jesus salvation.

Here is a mystery: the Lord Jesus Christ considers us His body on the earth. One day He will come and we will be as His Bride, made one with God forever. We are His Body. We are His Bride. His promise is yet to come. It is an analogy of union with God so much that we are ONE with Him. There is no ending to that river of God – the Holy Spirit – throughout eternity we can be learning of God in His beauty. We can be ruling and reigning with Him in the earth. We can be living in that place of total communion with Him. He is the source of all wisdom. We will be living in glory forever with Him. We can have an aspect of that glory now as He lives in us and through us. Christ in you, the hope of glory (Colossians 1: 27).

The desire of my heart is for more of God. I want more of God in me so that the Word of God is much a part of me that I become as a living epistle. I want the engrafted Word of God to be so much a part of the Church that the glory of God fills the Church. I want the Church to shine so brightly that all the earth would notice and there would be revival such as the earth has never seen, with people getting saved, healed delivered etc. I pray for worldwide evangelism and multitudes coming to know Jesus Christ.

CONCLUSION

I want to conclude as I would should I be sharing this word with you face to face. Lay hands on yourself and pray for yourself. I am praying in agreement with you that God will reveal more of Himself to you and draw you into closer relationship with Him.

PRAYER

I pray for the readers for further desire to come to know you, O God. O, that they would desire more of you God. That they would desire to want you as much as they want life itself. Release people to pray, to seek you, to pursue you, to know you. Release angels to remove hindrances that would try to stop their freedom: I pray for the outpouring of the Holy Spirit in the Church.

Release apostles, prophets, evangelists, pastors and teachers. Release people in spheres of society to shine as lights for Christ in Business, in Family, in the Church, in the Media, in Entertainment, in Government, in Education, in the Economy. Release people in Health Care and Technology who would bring you glory. Use people in the Body of Christ to be more than excellent in all they do so others would want to know the reason: that we might have opportunity to lead them to Christ.

O God, I pray reveal yourself by drawing all the members of the Body of Christ into intimate relationship with you. Draw us your church unto yourself. Fill us with your Hioly Spirit so strong that the gifts of the Spirit would manifest and the fruits of righteousness can be evident in our daily lives. O God I pray reveal yourself through your Church. Let there be a mighty outpouring of the Holy Spirit in Africa, in Asia, in the Middle East, in Israel, in South America, in North America, in the Pacific Rim, in Australia and New Zealand, throughout all of Europe. O God, you promised that the gospel would be preached in all the earth. Release angels to remove hindrances so that people can be released to preach and teach Christ. God ignite passion in me for You, for your Church, for those who do not yet know you. Amen.

O God, I pray, encourage, build up, strengthen, and release people to give themselves wholly to you whatever their job may be so that you can use them. Reveal your glory by manifesting your presence in their lives. Cut off bad influences from their lives; give them friends of like precious faith, people who will encourage them to seek you for the best you can give them in life. Let them desire you more than anything. Let them press into know you and let them be transformed from glory to glory. Raise up Apostles, Prophets, Pastors, Evangelists, Teachers to serve you and to teach and build up the Body of Christ. Use them in their serving gifts, their giving gifts, their leadership gifts; let them show your mercy. Let them be zealous for you more than anything. Give them desire to be used by you, to be consecrated to you that your will could be done on earth, so that your kingdom may come. Amen.

Prayer for you to Stir Up Your Spiritual Gifts

O God, I stir up the gift of faith within me. According to your words to Timothy, I stir up the gifts of God. I stir the gift of working of Miracles. I stir the gifts to healings. I stir the gifts of word of wisdom, word of knowledge and discerning of spirits. I stir the gifts of tongues and interpretation of tongues. O Holy Spirit pray in me and through me and for me so that I may pray your will to be done, your kingdom to come on earth as it is in heaven. I stir the gift of teaching and preaching. I stir the gifts of leadership and encouragement. I stir the gift of serving and of giving. Make me a giver after your own heart. I stir the gift of mercy that I may show the mercy of God towards other.

I stir up my faith in the releasing of these gifts in my life today. I pray that I may have opportunity to use these gifts and talents for your glory. O God fill me to overflowing that I may serve you this day. Give me divine connections that Christ might be glorified. Amen.

Other Books by Chris Legebow

Available on Amazon.ca Amazon.com or Amazon.ca or Kindle
Or the Create Space webstore.

The Anointing: the Glory of God. Living Word. 2017.

Discovering and Using your Spiritual Gifts. Living Word. 2016.

Living Life Fully: Knowing your Purpose. Living Word. 2016.

Kinds of Prayer. Knowing Them and Using Them Effectively.: Living Word. 2016.

The High Calling: Life Worth Living. Living Word. 2016.

ABOUT THE AUTHOR

Chris Legebow is a Christian Professor of English and Communications. She has taught at the elementary, high school and College and University levels. She has ministered in her local churches in intercessory prayer, teaching Sunday school and other Christian Doctrine classes to children and youths. She has preached to congregations and given her testimony. Although she was not raised in a Christian home, she came to know Jesus Christ as her Saviour and LORD while she was studying in University. This radically transformed her life in terms of priorities and commitment. She has a strong passion for the great commission – that Jesus Christ would be preached throughout all the earth believing that it a major sign of the LORD's return. She has been a part of several different types of full gospel charismatic churches but has also gained much of her insight and enlightenment from Christian Media and broadcasting. She hopes to continue ministering, serving, interceding and giving and teaching until the LORD returns.